11-99

Tom McGowen

GERMANY'S LIGHTNING WAR

PANZER DIVISIONS OF WORLD WAR II

TWENTY-FIRST CENTURY BOOKS

Brookfield, Connecticut

Cover and book designed by Joan O'Connor.

Cover photograph courtesy of Bilderdienst Suddeutscher Verlag7
Photographs courtesy of Corbis-Bettmann: p. 4; UPI/Corbis-Bettmann: pp. 8, 13, 41;
© Bildarchiv Preussischer Kulturbesitz, Berlin: pp. 9, 48, 63; Hulton Getty/Liaison Agency:
pp. 15, 18, 44; AP/Wide World Photos: p. 22; Bilderdienst Suddeutscher Verlag: pp. 24,
30, 33, 35, 59; Archive Photos: p. 26 (© Scott Swanson); Ullstein Bilderdienst, Berlin: 50,
52, 58, 61;

Library of Congress Cataloging in Publication Data

McGowen, Tom.
Germany's lightning war: Panzer divisions of World War II /
Tom McGowen.
p. cm.—(Military might)
Includes bibliographical references and index.
Summary: Discusses the development and action of German tank
units in World War II, covering specific battles and the changes
that tanks brought to warfare in general.
ISBN 0-7613-1511-X (lib. bdg.)
1. World War, 1939-1945—Tank warfare—Juvenile literature.
2. World War, 1939-1945—Germany—Juvenile literature. [1. World War,
1939-1945—Tank warfare. 2. World War, 1939-1945—Germany.]
I. Title. II. Series.
D796 .M34 1999 940.54'1–dc21   98-44009 CIP AC

Published by Twenty-First Century Books
A Division of The Millbrook Press, Inc.
2 Old New Milford Road
Brookfield, Connecticut 06804

Contents

Chapter 1

THE NEW WEAPON

In the year 1916, a 400-mile long stretch of barren landscape, scarred and mangled by countless explosions, ran in a winding zigzag through the countries of Belgium and France. On each side of this area of desolation were continuous lines of trenches; deep ditches dug into the earth, in which crouched the soldiers of opposing armies—the armies of Belgium, France, and Great Britain on one side, the army of Germany on the other. The terrible war, now known as World War I, had been raging for a little more than two years.

Here in France and Belgium the war was a stalemate, a situation in which neither side could win. Over the years, both sides had made many attacks on the others' trenches and had gained nothing. The soldiers in the trenches were protected by the earth, with only their heads showing, while the attacking soldiers were completely in the open. Fences of tangled barbed wire stretched in front of the lines of trenches, providing a bar-

German soldiers in a trench in World War I. Machine guns were placed at strategic points along the trench.

5

rier that charging men could not get through. At intervals in the trenches there were machine guns, set up so their fire could crisscross with each other, in hails of bullets that sliced through the attackers from two directions. Some distance behind the trenches was the artillery; clusters of cannons that could send hundreds of projectiles, called shells, screaming through the air to explode among the charging soldiers. Thus, an attack against trenches was almost suicide, and tens of thousands of men were killed and wounded every time such an attack was made. By the end of twenty-four months of the war, the commanders on both sides knew that to make a "breakthrough" and somehow smash through the enemy's lines, some special effort or weapon was needed.

The weapons of that time were not, of course, much like the weapons of today. There were no such things as guided missiles, nor helicopter gunships, nor jet planes, nor assault rifles. In 1916 the average infantryman (foot soldier) carried a rifle that held five to ten bullets that could only be fired one at a time. After each shot, the man had to pull back a lever that caused the empty cartridge to be ejected, then push it forward again to load another cartridge into the firing chamber. Machine guns could fire from three hundred to five hundred bullets a minute. Artillery pieces (cannons) could shoot from ten to twenty-five explosive shells a minute, to a distance of about 5 miles. There were airplanes, armed with machine guns and driven by propellers, that had a top speed of around 100 miles an hour. To fight off air attacks by planes, armies had cannons called antiaircraft guns, that fired shells up into the sky, where they exploded. Most armies made use of what were called armored cars; basically just a large automobile covered with bulletproof armor and armed with one or two machine guns. These vehicles were of no use for attacking trenches, and they could not even move on muddy ground that had been churned up by artillery explosions. But they were useful for scouting, because they couldn't be damaged by rifle or machine-gun fire and could defend themselves very well against small units of infantry or cavalry.

There were, as yet, no tanks.

But on a hot day in September 1916, German soldiers in trenches south of the French town of Bapaume, near the Somme River, stared in astonishment at what they beheld. Advancing toward them were hordes of British soldiers, and here and there among the soldiers were strange big, bulky objects that seemed to be metal-covered vehicles of some sort, moving on tractor treads. With ponderous slowness the things pushed right through the barbed-wire entanglements and headed menacingly toward the trenches.

In the face of these unknown monstrous machines many Germans simply lost their courage and fled. Others opened up with rifles and machine-gun fire, but the bullets merely *pinged* harmlessly off the things. And the vehicles were firing back, with machine guns and small cannons that jutted out of their sides! More Germans fled, others threw down their rifles, raised their hands, and surrendered.

The rumbling metal monsters were, of course, armored fighting vehicles—tanks. They had been developed by the British Army, and got the name tank because they were shipped from Britain to France in wooden cartons stamped "tank" in an attempt to trick German spies into thinking they were merely some kind of mobile water container. The use of this new weapon, although it did terrify many German soldiers into running away or surrendering, did not cause the breakthrough that British generals had hoped for, but it did show what tanks might be capable of doing.

In time, both the French and Germans were building tanks of their own design. The French called their tanks *chars de combat*, meaning "combat vehicles," while the Germans called theirs *panzerkampfwagen*, or "armored battle vehicle." Tanks were used

The first photograph of a British tank in action shows a heavily armored vehicle climbing out of a shell crater in France late in the year 1916.

again, by both sides in other battles of World War I, but because they were a completely new weapon, generals were not quite sure how best to use them. Thus, they were never really used well and never accomplished much.

The war ended in 1918, with the defeat of Germany and its allies, Austria and Turkey, by the forces of France, Great Britain, Belgium, Italy, and the United States. As soon as the fighting stopped, each nation's army began to carefully study everything that had happened during the war, to find out how their weapons and methods of warfare had worked. One of the things they all looked at very closely was this new weapon, the tank. In every army there were a few men, mostly young, low-ranked officers, who saw in tanks the promise of a major decisive weapon, and who began to puzzle out new ways of using tanks more effectively.

In all the armies of the world at that time, soldiers were organized in basic units known as regiments. An infantry regi-

Early German tanks were gigantic battle wagons as can be seen in this photograph from 1918.

ment consisted of about 3,000 foot soldiers; an artillery regiment had some 36 cannons and about 1,400 men to operate them; a cavalry regiment had about 700 men and horses. The main fighting force of an army was called a division, which was generally formed of three infantry regiments, two artillery regiments, small units of engineers (builders of bridges, roads, and other things), medical personnel, and men who drove wagons containing supplies and ammunition. Groups of divisions were formed into units called corps, and corps were formed into armies. As far as tanks were concerned, they really didn't fit into any of these organizations. There were no tank regiments, much less tank divisions.

But in Britain, where the tank had been invented, there were a number of young British Army officers who believed that tanks should actually become their army's *main* weapon, and who dreamed of tank regiments, tank divisions, and even tank *armies*. These men felt that the kind of breakthrough generals had sought in World War I could be made by huge numbers of tanks smashing through enemy lines of defense and moving at top speed to capture or destroy enemy headquarters, wiping out communications from commanders to their troops, causing panic and terror. This could make whole armies collapse, insisted the tank enthusiasts.

However, older officers with greater authority and power, who firmly believed that wars could only be won as they always had been, by the action of infantry or cavalry, scoffed at the idea of tanks as a main weapon. Some even regarded tanks as a "freak" weapon, that was of no real use at all. And it was these men who made the decision about how tanks should be used. There would be no such thing as a tank division, these British military leaders agreed. They said that tanks would be used by the British Army only to support (back up) infantry or cavalry.

Several firms in Britain began to manufacture tanks, and by 1936, two main types were being produced. The little Mark VIB was a light tank with only about 0.5 inch of armor and a speed of 35 miles an hour. It was armed with two machine guns and operated by a three-man crew. This became the British Army's cavalry tank. For the infantry, a heavy tank known as the Matilda was selected. A type known as the Mark I was produced first; it had almost 2.5 inches of armor, one machine gun, and a snail-like speed of only 8 miles an hour. A second model, the Mark II, had more than 3 inches of armor, was armed with a cannon as well as a machine gun, and had a considerably better speed of 15 miles an hour. But that was more than enough to keep up with foot soldiers in an attack, which was the only job that heavy tanks would do as far as most of the British generals were concerned.

The many cavalry regiments of the British Army gradually changed over entirely from horses to light tanks. A cavalry regiment soon consisted of three squadrons of fifty-eight tanks each, plus a "headquarters" squadron with four or five tanks to carry the higher officers. These regiments were supposed to be the "eyes" of the army; scouting forces whose job would be to search for the enemy, find out as much as possible, and report what they found. They were only to fight when they had to, to protect themselves.

And so, the British Army fitted the new weapon into its plans for fighting the next war—big, well-armored but slow tanks to help out the infantry; small, fast, lightly armored tanks to take the place of horses. Nothing more needed to be done, the generals agreed.

Chapter 2

FRANCE BUILDS A WALL

After World War I, the Army of France not only had to decide how to use tanks, but also how to improve its whole way of fighting a war. The leaders of the French Army and government were convinced that their only hope of preventing another invasion by Germany (which had invaded France twice during the previous fifty years) was to create a vast defensive barrier of some kind. In the 1920s, France began construction of what became known as the Maginot Line, a long line of fortifications stretching along the entire border between France and Germany, from the edge of the tiny country of Luxembourg down to the border of Switzerland. Named after André Maginot, the French minister of war who conceived it, the line was a string of concrete and steel forts armed with large, long-range cannons, concealed machine gun and antitank gun emplacements, deep ditches, barbed-wire entanglements, areas of buried explosive mines, and obstacles that resembled rows of giant jagged teeth, designed to tear the treads off any tanks that tried to get through them.

The Maginot Line, a string of forts, stretched through the French country-side from Luxembourg to Switzerland.

The forts were masterpieces of the technology of the time. They extended down several stories below the ground and were built to withstand heavy bombing and artillery fire. They were well lit, air-conditioned, and equipped with running water and top-grade plumbing. Electric-powered trains ran through them, so that soldiers could be whisked from one point to another in event of attack. It was firmly believed, not only in France but throughout most of the world, that it would be impossible for any army to break through the Maginot Line. A newsreel (film news documentary) presented in American movie theaters during 1939, showed the barking cannons of Maginot forts during test firings, while the rich voice of the commentator announced: "These guns say, in no uncertain terms, they shall not pass!"

But, of course, the Maginot Line was essentially just a *wall*, like the Great Wall of China. The trouble with a wall is that it has two ends, and an enemy can come *around* either end. One end of the Maginot Line rested against the border of Switzerland, and to get around it, the Germans would have to go through Swiss territory. Of course, this would mean war with Switzerland, so that wasn't something the Germans were likely to do. Nevertheless, the French military leaders knew that the Swiss end of the Maginot Line was not completely safe, and they decided that if war broke out with Germany, a strong force would have to be put there to guard against a German attack through Switzerland. Thus, they would be prepared at that end.

The other end of the line was set at the edge of the Ardennes Mountains, a rugged range of 1,600-foot high mountains extending from Luxembourg into Belgium. They are covered by a vast thick forest of giant oak and beech trees, and split in many places by deep ravines through which rush fast-moving rivers. It would be impossible, it seemed, for an army to move with any speed through the Ardennes Forest on the narrow, winding roads that were often blocked by fallen trees. And so, French military leaders considered the Ardennes a "natural" defensive barrier. No one could get around the Maginot Line by going through the Ardennes, they agreed, so that end of the line was safe.

That left only the border between France and Belgium as a place where German armies could get into France. But if the Germans struck through Belgium and tried to swing down into

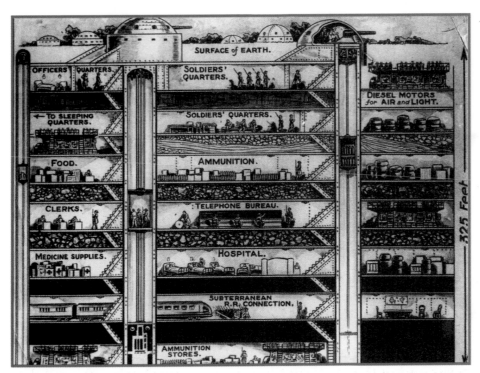

The forts of the Maginot Line were technological marvels, sitting atop underground rooms and connected to each other via an underground railway.

France, as they had done at the beginning of World War I, France would be ready. The French had a plan for moving up into Belgium, joining with the Belgian Army and with the forces that they knew would quickly be sent from Britain, and striking a blow that would drive the Germans reeling back in retreat.

But an army that depends on a wall to hold off an enemy is an army that is thinking only of *defense*. With a fortress protecting its border, and a plan to wait for an invasion before even moving its armies, France was obviously planning to fight a purely defensive war. The commanders of the French Army readily admitted this. "How can anyone believe that we are still thinking of the offensive (attack) when we have spent so many billions to establish a fortified frontier?" asked one of the generals. As a result of this kind of thinking, the French attitude toward tanks was to use them only as a defensive weapon.

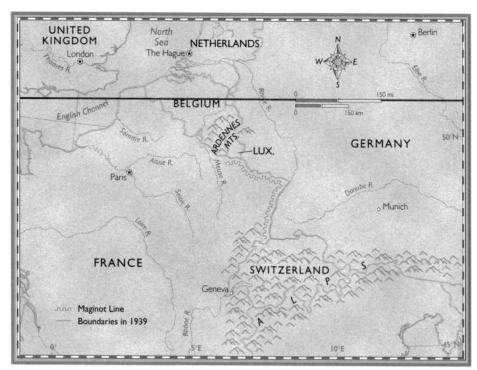

The Maginot Line

Of course, like Great Britain, France also had some officers who hoped that tanks would become France's main weapon and who dreamed of tank divisions. But almost no attention was paid to them. Soon after the end of World War I, the French General Staff decided on the kinds of tanks it intended to have—big, heavily armored, slow-moving tanks to help the infantry, and small, light, quick-moving tanks to help the cavalry. Just as in the British Army, tanks were to be strictly a support weapon.

In 1929 the French began manufacturing test models of what was to be the army's main battle tank. In 1935 full production of this tank began. Known as the Char B.1, it was a large heavy tank that resembled the tanks of World War I. With armor almost 2.5 inches thick, it weighed 32 tons and had a speed of 17.5 miles an hour. It was well armed, with an antitank gun—a type of cannon that fired a solid projectile with such speed it could rip through tank armor—as well as a cannon for firing on troops, and two machine guns. The new tank was operated by a crew of four men.

The French experimented with a number of light tanks and finally came up with two, known as the H–35 and R–35, which were much alike. One weighed almost ten tons and the other a bit more than eleven. Both tanks had two-man crews and were armed with one antitank gun and one machine gun. Both were heavily armored and rather slow, with a speed of 17.5 miles an hour for the H–35 and only 12.5 miles an hour for the R–35.

France also produced what was called a medium (middle) tank, known as the S–35. Almost as heavily armored as the Char B.1, it had a much better speed of about 25 miles an hour. It was armed with an antitank gun and had a three-man crew.

Armored cars and half-track vehicles were also built, mainly for the cavalry. A half-track was an armored trucklike vehicle with wheels on the front and tank treads on the back, so it could be steered like a car but could also climb over rough ground like a tank. Half-tracks were used to carry foot soldiers into combat and to pull large heavy cannons.

In the early 1930s, the French cavalry began adding motorized troops to its divisions—soldiers carried in half-tracks. Eventually, the French had cavalry divisions that had 2,000 soldiers on horses, 1,500 men in half-track vehicles and armored cars, and 45 light tanks. Each division also had an artillery regiment of twenty-four cannons, but as a result of incredibly foolish planning, the guns were pulled by horses instead of by vehicles, which meant that they usually got left far behind when the division was on the move.

These "mechanized" cavalry divisions finally led the French Army commanders to consider organizing an all-mechanized division, and in 1935, France put together what was the world's first tank division. It was known as a DLM, standing for *Division*

The French Army's main battle tank was the heavyweight Char B.I.

Légère Méchanique, or Light Mechanized Division. A DLM had 84 light tanks and 84 medium tanks, for a total of 168; plus 2,250 motorized infantrymen in trucks and half-tracks, 36 cannons, and 12 antitank cannons. A DLM was not intended to be a hard-hitting offensive unit, but was designed to be used only for scouting out ahead of an army, and any fighting it might do was to be purely defensive. Thus, France, like Great Britain, spurned the idea of having any such thing as a "heavy" armored division that would be a hard-hitting offensive weapon. The Commander-in-Chief of the French Army, General Maurice Gamelin, argued against building any such divisions for France.

French military leaders also ignored the possibilities of certain kinds of military aircraft. At that time, some nations were experimenting with a type of aircraft known as a dive bomber, which could dive almost straight down at its target and drop a large bomb from a height of only a few hundred feet, for a direct hit. Although a French aircraft designer had built a dive bomber, air force generals had been uninterested in it, so the French Air Force had no dive bombers. There were also only 150 medium and heavy bombers—planes that flew over their targets and dropped bombs from a great height—in the entire French Air Force. The air force did have a fairly large number of fighter planes, the main job of which was to attack enemy bombers or defend their own bombers, but they were not at all as fast and maneuverable as the fighter planes of some other nations.

Despite all these shortcomings, most of the world's military experts of the 1930s regarded the French Army as the world's best, right up to the beginning of World War II. The French General Staff agreed. General Gamelin stated that he could not see any weaknesses in the French Army. Thus, like Great Britain, France considered itself well ready for any future war it might have to fight.

Chapter 3

THE GERMAN PANZER DIVISIONS

At the end of World War I much of France and Belgium lay in ruins, while Germany's towns and cities had suffered hardly any damage at all. Most of the victorious nations, particularly France, were determined to make the Germans pay for the destruction they had caused, and to prevent them from ever being able to make war again. Harsh penalties were imposed on Germany. It was forced to give up large amounts of territory and to pay huge sums of money. It had to sign agreements to reduce the size of the German Army to no more than 100,000 men, and never again to have a navy or air force. And Germany was ordered not to build any tanks. From being a major power, Germany was reduced to the rank of a second-rate nation.

The main purpose of an army is to defend its country, and now the small, weak army left to Germany had the problem of trying to work out ways of defending Germany in the event it was attacked. Officers noted for their intelligence and ability were given the task of studying various problems that would have to be overcome in order to make the little army as effective as possible. One such problem was, of course, what to do about tanks. The officer selected to work on this problem was a captain by the name of Heinz Guderian.

Captain Guderian had fought in World War I and he had once been in a battle that was won by French tanks supported by a large number of airplanes. He had been tremendously impressed by this, and now that he had the responsibility of trying to put together some kind of mechanized force for Germany, he felt he should learn as much about tanks as possible. He got hold of all the books about tanks he could find, and began to soak up information.

Guderian soon came to the conclusion that a mixture of tanks and troops carried in motorized vehicles, supported by airplanes to bomb and machine gun the enemy, could provide an advantage in combat that might give a small army an edge over a bigger one. Over a period of time he worked out organizations that combined units of tanks with units of troops in trucks, on motorcycles, and in armored cars. Germany was prohibited from having any actual tanks, so Guderian had dummy tanks made, out of cars and trucks covered with "pretend" armor of cardboard or canvas. (These sometimes suffered damage from German schoolchildren, who poked holes in the cardboard or canvas with pencil points so they could peek in.) The dummy tanks were useless for actual combat, of course, but they could move just as fast as a real tank, and this enabled Guderian to test his tank ideas in "war games," in which his tank units "fought" against other troops, with umpires carefully watching to judge such things as casualties and damage to vehicles. In this way, Guderian gained considerable information about what tanks and motorized troops could do under combat conditions.

By 1929, Guderian, like some British and French officers, was convinced that tanks, instead of infantry or cavalry, should be the main fighting force of an army. He, too, dreamed of tank divisions, which he visualized as fast-moving combinations of

German Captain Heinz Guderian tested his ideas about tank warfare by using dummy tanks like these in war games.

hundreds of tanks, motorized infantry, and motorized artillery (cannons towed by trucks or half-track vehicles in which the men who operated the cannons rode). The generals in command would ride in tanks or armored cars up at the front of the division, where they could see what was going on, and they would have radio contact with the air force in order to call for quick bombing attacks on the division's opponents. Such panzer (armor) divisions could score tremendous victories, Guderian felt sure, by smashing through an enemy's front line and speeding straight to his unprotected rear areas, cutting off supplies and reinforcements for units at the front. A few other German officers believed as Guderian did, but most did not.

Just as in the British and French armies, the older German generals, the men who controlled the army, did not think of tanks as a major weapon and wanted to use them only as support for the infantry and cavalry. For these men, like their British and French counterparts, the idea of tank divisions was preposterous.

But suddenly, Guderian gained some powerful help. In 1933 the political party known as the National Socialist German Workers Party, the Nazis, gained control of the government of Germany, and its leader, Adolf Hitler, became head of the government. Hitler was known to be extremely interested in the army and its weapons and equipment. Soon after he took power, the generals in charge of developing the army's weapons arranged to give him a giant demonstration of new weapons and tactics. Heinz Guderian was delighted to find that he was going to be given half an hour during the demonstration to show off the skills and abilities of his tank and motorized infantry units. When the time came, his motorcycle troops roared across the field and rapidly took up battle positions, truck-towed antitank guns were quickly set up for firing, and armored cars darted here and there, simulating attacks. Hitler watched this with his eyes shining. "That's what I need!" he exclaimed. "That's what I want to have!"

The promises that Germany had been forced to make after its surrender in World War I—to keep its army at only 100,000 men, to have no navy or air force, and to build no tanks—had caused great bitterness among the German people. One of the main reasons that the Nazi party had been voted into control of the government was that it had pledged to ignore those promises, and turn Germany into a great power once again. Soon after his election as head of the government, Adolf Hitler gave a speech in which he hinted that he intended to expand and reequip the German armed forces. Heinz Guderian was not completely happy about having the Nazi party in control of the

A battalion of tanks maneuvers before a vast audience during a panzer division review in the German city of Nuremberg in 1936.

government, but like all the other officers of the German Army he was glad that Germany's military forces were to be restored. He was also elated that the man who now controlled everything in Germany, Adolf Hitler, was in agreement with him about the need for panzer divisions.

In 1934, Guderian, now a colonel, was appointed Chief of Staff of the army's new Motorized Troop Command Staff, a group of officers selected to solve all the problems of putting together an actual panzer division. Most of the older generals who had opposed the idea of panzer divisions were replaced by men who were more agreeable to it. In March 1935, Hitler officially announced to the world that Germany was going to increase the size of its army above the 100,000-man limit that had been imposed on it, and was also going to begin producing the kinds of weapons it had been told it couldn't have. By the summer of 1935, Guderian and his fellow officers were able to put together a panzer training division.

Supposedly, there weren't any tanks in Germany for such an organization, because Germany hadn't been allowed to build them. But the Germans had been cheating. Under the pretense of manufacturing tractors for farm use, German industry had developed a small, lightly armored tank armed with two machine guns. Known as the *Panzerkampfwagen* I, or PzKpfw I, it had a two-man crew and a top speed of 25 miles an hour. It was really designed only to be a vehicle for training tank crews, so it became the main tank of the panzer training division. However, a few tanks of a newer type, the PzKpfw II, were also produced and given to the division. The PzKpfw II's armor was twice as thick as that of the PzKpfw I, and it was armed with one machine gun plus a small antitank gun. It had the same speed as the PzKpfw I and was operated by a crew of three; a driver, a gunner who handled the antitank gun, and a commander, who also handled the machine gun.

Germany also began building armored cars and half-tracks for panzer divisions. As well as carrying troops and towing cannons, half-tracks could be used as vehicles for generals and other officers to ride in. Armored cars were being formed into scouting units for the panzer divisions. Much faster than tanks, they could move far ahead of the division and radio back information about everything they saw. They could also fight, if need be.

By October 1935 three actual panzer divisions had been formed, one of them commanded by Colonel Guderian. A German panzer division was designed to consist of two tank regiments with about 280 tanks; an artillery regiment of 36 cannons and 36 antitank cannons, all towed by trucks; two infantry regiments (4,500 men) in trucks; a battalion of motorcycle troops (about 780 men); a scouting battalion of armored cars and motorcycle troops, and units of antiaircraft guns, engi-

A German tank trooper stands proudly in front of his PzKpfw I.

neers, medical personnel, and supply troops. The first panzer divisions did not have all these things they were supposed to have, but everything was slowly added as time went on.

The military buildup of Germany was proceeding in other ways as well. The German *Luftwaffe* (air force) had been formed, and shipyards were beginning to build warships. Germany was well behind both Great Britain and France in its ability to fight a war, but it was catching up fast!

Chapter 4

THE ROAD TO WAR

Hitler began to show signs of belligerence. In 1936 he sent German troops marching into the Rhineland, one of the pieces of territory that had been taken from Germany after World War I, to repossess it. The Rhineland was under the control of France and Great Britain. The German generals held their breath, for these nations had large, well-equipped armies, and if they sent troops into the Rhineland to challenge Hitler's move, the German force would have been overwhelmed. But France and Great Britain did nothing, and the Rhineland became part of Germany once again. Hitler had gambled and won.

In February 1938, Hitler took the title of Commander-in-Chief of the German Armed Forces, and removed a number of high-ranking generals from duty. However, Heinz Guderian was promoted to the rank of lieutenant general and given command of the 16th Army Corps, which was formed of Germany's first three panzer divisions. Two more panzer divisions, the 4th and 5th, were formed during 1938, and the *Luftwaffe*, which was to be an essential partner in the tactics of the panzer divisions, reached 2,900 planes.

Hitler now began to throw all restraint aside. In Austria, which like Germany had been humbled after World War I, many people openly admired what Hitler and the Nazis were doing in Germany, and wanted Austria to become part of Germany. This gave Hitler an excuse. On March 10, 1938, forces of the German Army, including Guderian's panzer corps, marched into Austria where they were met by crowds of cheering people. With the agreement of the Austrian government, which Hitler had bluffed and threatened, Austria now became part of Germany. This, of course, made the Austrian Army part of the German Army, enlarging the German Army considerably.

In one of Germany's other neighbors, Czechoslovakia (now the two separate countries of Slovakia and the Czech Republic), there were also people who wanted union with Germany. Most, however, did not. But again, by means of threats, bullying, and bluff, Hitler managed to gain the large slice of Czechoslovakian territory in which most of those who wanted to become part of Germany lived. On October 4 this region, known as the Sudetenland, was occupied by German troops and officially became part of Germany.

The year of 1939 dawned. It was now twenty-one years since World War I had ended, and the effectiveness of weapons had increased quite a lot during that time. Military airplanes were still driven by propellers, but now they flew at speeds of 250 to 350 miles an hour. The average cannon could now hurl a shell 7 to 10 miles. Machine guns fired at a rate of eight hundred bullets a minute, and many soldiers were now armed with semiautomatic rifles that could fire in bursts, like a machine gun, as well as one bullet at a time. All armies had antitank guns, antiaircraft guns, armored cars, half-tracks, and tanks.

By this time Hitler seemed convinced that he could do just about what he wanted and Great Britain and France would do

In October 1938, Germany occupied part of Czechoslovakia called the Sudetenland. Many residents there welcomed the arrival of Hitler's troops.

nothing to stop him. In March there was unrest in Czechoslovakia and the danger of civil war flared. Under the pretense of keeping the peace, Hitler sent the German Army in, and all of Czechoslovakia now became part of Germany. One of the things Germany gained from this was the equipment and weapons of the Czech Army, which included 469 medium tanks—each armed with an antitank cannon and two machine guns, covered with an inch of armor, and capable of a speed of 25 miles an hour. Thus, Germany's panzer divisions gained many excellent new tanks. There were soon six panzer divisions, for a new one was created in April. Although it was only the sixth, it was officially designated the 10th.

Hitler now turned his attention to another neighbor, Poland. After World War I, a section of territory containing the important German port city of Danzig (now Gdansk) had been taken from Germany and given to Poland. Hitler demanded that this now be returned. Poland refused, and made ready to defend itself. Clearly, war was about ready to break out. Great Britain and France announced that they would go to Poland's aid if Germany attacked it. They also tried to get a promise from the Soviet Union (now Russia and the Baltic States) that it, too, would aid the Poles.

Among officers of the German Army the mood was grim. If Hitler embarked on a war against Poland, Germany might well find itself fighting Great Britain and France in the west and Poland and Russia in the east—a war on two fronts. A two-front war of this sort was the terror of the German Army; this was what had caused Germany's defeat in World War I.

But then, on August 23, Hitler made the astounding announcement that the German government had signed a nonaggression pact—an agreement not to attack each other—with the Soviet Union. This was astounding, because the political systems of the two nations, fascism in Germany and communism in the Soviet Union, were totally opposed to each other, and each sought the other's destruction. But with this agreement, Hitler was now free to carry out his plans against Poland without any fear of a two-front war involving the powerful forces of the Soviet Union. Eight days later, in the early morning darkness of 4:45 A.M. on September 1, the German Army began to move across the Polish border. World War II was about to begin, and Heinz Guderian's panzer divisions were about to be tested in battle.

Chapter 5

THE CONQUEST OF POLAND

Germany attacked Poland with sixty divisions, six of which were panzer divisions and four of which were "light" divisions that had some tanks. Altogether, the Germans had nearly 2,600 tanks. This force was formed into five armies that were organized into two groups designated as Army Group North and Army Group South. Most of the German soldiers who made up these armies wore a battle uniform consisting of a grayish-green coat with dark green collar and shoulder straps, and gray pants tucked into black, knee-high leather boots. Their metal helmets were a dull grayish green. But the men that made up the tank crews of the panzer divisions had a distinct all-black uniform and peaked cap, trimmed with silver. The German tanks were a darkish gray in color, with white crosses on their sides or turrets to show their nationality (a cross had been the German military emblem for hundreds of years).

Against the German forces Poland could put only forty infantry divisions, eleven brigades (half divisions) of horsed cavalry, and two small units totaling about seven hundred small

The Polish Army depended heavily upon old-fashioned cavalry forces.

tanks. Much of the Polish equipment, such as cannons and vehicles, was more than twenty years old, left over from World War I.

Poland also had only 397 military airplanes, of which just 159 were fighter planes, whereas the German *Luftwaffe* had put together a force of 1,600 aircraft for the invasion: heavy bombers, dive bombers, and fighters. On the morning of the invasion the sky was foggy, but by early afternoon the fog had lifted and the *Luftwaffe* went into action. Flights of bombers roared up into the sky and headed for their targets, the airfields of the Polish Air Force. Scores of Polish planes were caught on the ground and destroyed in fiery blasts. Most of the fighter planes that managed to get up were no match for the swift, modern German fighters that accompanied the bombers. In a few days the *Luftwaffe* achieved what is known as air supremacy, meaning that there were no longer enough Polish planes left to be any threat.

General Guderian was in command of the 19th Army Corps, which was formed of the 3rd Panzer Division and two divisions of motorized (truck-carried) infantry. His panzer division, as well as the other panzer divisions of the German force, contained some of the newest German tanks; the PzKpfw III, with an antitank gun, and the PzKpfw IV, with a large cannon for use against troops.

The three divisions of Guderian's corps crossed the Polish border in the morning mist, with Guderian at the front of the 3rd Panzer Division in a half-track command vehicle. His orders were to move straight ahead, cross the Brahe River, a small stream some 150 miles from the border, and proceed on to the big Vistula River. This part of Poland was perfect tank country, a flat plain. By about three o'clock in the afternoon the scouting units of the panzer division reached the banks of the Brahe and found that the bridge across the river was defended by Polish troops in trenches on the opposite bank. Guderian arrived at about five o'clock and ordered the division's motorcycle battalion to go farther downstream where they couldn't be seen, cross the stream in inflated rubber boats, and attack the entrenched troops from the side. While the Polish troops were trying to fight off this attack, Guderian sent the division tanks roaring across the bridge. The Polish soldiers surrendered. By six o'clock the entire division was across the river and speeding toward the Vistula, which was reached early in the night.

The next day the three divisions of Guderian's corps moved forward side by side, some miles apart from one another, and each ran into heavy fighting. The tanks and trucks moved so quickly they often caught enemy units by surprise. A Polish artillery regiment was overrun by the tanks and completely wiped out, and columns of Polish trucks and wagons carrying supplies and bridge-building equipment were caught unawares on roads and completely destroyed. By September 3, the 19th Corps had surrounded and eliminated all the enemy units in front of it. The Poles had lost nearly three infantry divisions, a cavalry brigade, and hundreds of artillery pieces. Thousands of men had been taken prisoner.

The Polish Army was no match for the tanks of the German panzer divisions. The German conquest of Poland was accomplished in less than a month.

General Guderian and his troops did not know it, but they had fought in one of the first battles of World War II. After doing nothing about Germany's retaking of the Rhineland and its takeovers of Austria and Czechoslovakia, Great Britain and France had now declared war on Germany over the invasion of Poland. The war that was to become known as World War II had begun.

By now, Guderian had seen enough of his tanks in combat so that he was able to judge their successes and failures. Their speed and their armor had kept casualties quite light; only 150 men killed and 700 wounded out of the entire division. But it had become obvious that the tanks could do better if they had antitank guns that fired a larger projectile at a longer range.

The rest of the German forces, south of Guderian's corps,

were also steadily advancing, with the panzer divisions generally leading the way. The planes of the *Luftwaffe* operated closely with the army, bombing enemy troops to throw them into confusion before a German attack, and bombing and machine-gunning supply columns on roads and in towns.

The German *Stuka* dive bombers were particularly effective. Equipped with sirens that blared a loud terrifying shriek that added to the fright of the soldiers being attacked, they dived almost straight down at their targets, pulling up suddenly only a few hundred feet above the ground and dropping a 500-pound bomb that exploded with a deafening and devastating concussion. General Kutrzeba of the Polish Army said of such bombing, "It was Hell come to earth!" Troops generally fled rather than stay in place to be dive-bombed, and this often kept them from carrying out important tasks, such as the destruction of bridges to keep German troops from crossing a river.

The German plan for defeating Poland was what is called a pincers movement, in which a force advances in a long line, the ends of which gradually curl forward around the enemy force, eventually surrounding it and squeezing it together. By the sixth of September the ends of the pincers were beginning to curl. General Guderian's corps, at the head of the German Third and Fourth Armies, was coming down from the north behind the Polish lines, heading for the city of Brest-Litovsk, some 112 miles east of the Polish capital, Warsaw. The panzer divisions heading the Germans' southern forces were swinging up toward Warsaw. Because of the swift movement of the panzers the Polish forces were unable to stop what was happening to them. Amidst dead bodies and wrecked equipment left shattered and burning by the German dive-bombers, Polish soldiers watched helplessly as the German tanks and motorcycle troops came roaring at them.

The commanders of panzer units made daring and unexpected moves. General Ritter von Thoma, leading the tanks of

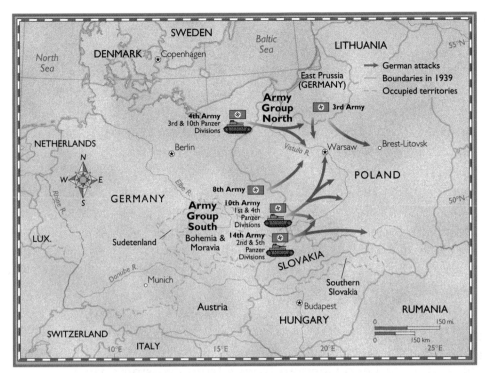

The Conquest of Poland

2nd Panzer Division, needed to move his force down into a valley. There was only a single narrow pass leading into the valley, and a strong force of Polish troops with numerous antitank guns was waiting for the Germans at the end of it. But instead of using the pass and risking the loss of many tanks, von Thoma took his tanks through a thick forest on a high ridge—which Polish commanders didn't believe he could possibly do—and came down into the valley *behind* the Poles, catching them by surprise and not losing a single tank.

On the fourteenth of September the leading units of Guderian's corps broke through the Polish line of fortified positions outside Brest-Litovsk and captured the city. Three days later, still moving southward, Guderian's corps met the leading units of the three German armies moving up from the south. The pincers movement was now completed, and the remains of the Polish forces in and around Warsaw were completely surrounded. Poland's defeat was sealed.

On September 19, more than 100,000 Polish soldiers, the remains of 19 infantry divisions and 3 cavalry brigades that had been fighting around Warsaw, surrendered. Over the next eight days the small areas where Polish troops were still holding out were cleaned up. By September 27, less than a month from the day it had been invaded, Poland was conquered. Polish army losses in killed and wounded were about 200,000 men, to German army losses of only 48,000!

Even though the Polish Army was outnumbered and poorly armed and equipped, the German conquest of Poland was a masterpiece of modern warfare. A perfect example of the new tactics that were to become known as *Blitzkrieg* ("Lightning War"), it provided many lessons. Perhaps most important of all, the Germans had found that panzer divisions could easily move *around* heavily defended positions and catch the defenders by surprise, simply by moving through places that the enemy believed tanks couldn't get through, such as forests.

The military leaders of Great Britain and France did not pay any attention to these lessons, however. Nor did they really pay any attention to the way the German panzer divisions had operated against Polish forces. They simply assumed that Poland had been easily beaten because it was outnumbered and not very well equipped. Said one French general smugly: "We are not Poles. It will not happen here." Thus, the armies of France and Great Britain remained unaware of the German "lightning war" tactics—the swift, terrorizing rush of the panzers, teamed up with the sky-clearing, earth-shattering force of the *Luftwaffe*. But these were the tactics that were going to be used against them.

Chapter 6

THE "PHONY WAR"

Many of the men in the army of France were "reservists," meaning that they were kept in reserve until a war actually began. They were really civilians, who had jobs, lived in houses or apartments, wore ordinary clothing most of the time, and only trained as soldiers for a few weeks of each year. As it became obvious that war with Germany was about to begin, these reservists were ordered to take their place as full-time soldiers. Those that were trained as "fortress" troops began to fill up the Maginot Line, and those trained as "field" soldiers joined the regiments they were assigned to. By the time France actually declared war on Germany, the French Army had sixty-seven field divisions in position along the French-Belgian border and behind the Maginot Line.

The men who made up these divisions were known by the nickname of *poilus* (PWAH loos), which means "bearded ones." Their metal helmets and uniforms—jacket, knee-length pants, leg wrappings, and a long overcoat—were a yellowish-brown color, and they carried rifles that fired five shots before reloading. One man in every "combat group" of twelve men carried a light machine gun that could fire five hundred shots a minute.

When France and Britain had declared war on Germany, Poland pleaded for help, begging the two allied nations to make an assault on Germany that would force the Germans to pull their troops out of Poland in order to defend their country. If the Allies *had* made a quick attack across the French-German border, Germany certainly would have been in extreme danger, facing an invasion with most of its troops out of the country. However, on the German side of the border was the Westwall, a series of underground fortifications, barbed wire, ditches, tank traps, and minefields, much like the Maginot Line. It had only been begun in 1936, and was not quite finished by the end of 1939, but the French military leaders nevertheless regarded it as a major barrier. All the French did was send a relatively small force of nine divisions moving slowly and cautiously over the border about 5 miles into Germany. Then, they quickly pulled back. Thus, the chance was lost, Poland fell, and the German troops began hurrying back into Germany, building up a greater and greater force that finally totaled ninety-three divisions facing the Allies. The French continued to build up their forces until they had some ninety-four divisions in nine armies that were organized into three army groups and a reserve force. Great Britain had sent five divisions to France, and more, including a tank brigade of one hundred big Matilda tanks, were on the way.

Now there began a strange time that became known as the "phony war," or, in Germany, as the *sitzkrieg*, meaning "sitting war." For months, absolutely nothing happened among French, British, and German land forces. French and German soldiers did not even shoot at one another when they were close enough to see one another's faces. French sentries "stood" guard seated on chairs, with their machine guns resting in the grass beside

This photo of a French soldier sitting on a road marker that says "Berlin, 632" (379 miles), was taken to show the confidence the French had that they would invade Germany and win the war.

them. In areas of land behind the forts of the Maginot Line, French soldiers started vegetable gardens!

Morale and discipline began to suffer badly in the French Army. After being told for years that France had the best army in the world, most French soldiers believed that France could not be beaten and that Germany would be easily defeated. The soldiers, particularly the reservists, did not feel a need to keep up their efficiency by doing a lot of training, and grumbled when they had to do any work. Among the troops in the Maginot Line there were many cases of men becoming drunk while they were on duty.

In Germany, however, things were very different. At Hitler's orders the German Army was preparing a smashing onslaught against France. The plan, which was mostly Hitler's, was to strike into the Netherlands and Belgium—both actually *neutral*, or non-enemy countries—making moves that would split the British and French forces apart when they came hurrying into Belgium according to their plan. Then, the German forces would push on to the coast, to capture seaports that could be used for an attack on Britain. It was not really a very good plan, but on January 10, 1940, Hitler ordered the attack on Belgium to be launched on the seventeenth, and the movement of troops began.

But then, suddenly, the order was canceled. One of those strange twists of fate that happen throughout history to change things had taken place. A German plane flying near the Belgian border got lost in a fog and had to make a crash-landing in Belgium. On the plane was a *Luftwaffe* officer who was carrying a copy of the complete plan for the German invasion! He tried unsuccessfully to destroy the papers, but they were taken from him by some Belgian soldiers and quickly brought to the attention of the commander of the Belgian Army. Thus, Belgium learned that it and the Netherlands were about to be invaded by the forces of Germany.

The Belgian commander notified the Allied commander, General Gamelin, and the Dutch. Gamelin notified the British government. The Belgian and Dutch armies began to move into position in their countries, and the French and British forces were rearranged.

It was obvious to Hitler and his generals that it was no longer possible to carry out the invasion as they had planned. But now Hitler came up with another idea—an invasion of Denmark and Norway.

There was actually sound reason for these new plans. Germany was buying quantities of iron, which was vital to its war needs, from Sweden, and the shipments came by sea through waters off the coast of Norway. Should Great Britain decide to have its navy spread explosive mines in those waters, the essential shipments would be cut off. But if Germany seized Norway this could be prevented, and seizing Denmark as well would give Germany a valuable air base for use against Britain. On April 2, Hitler ordered the invasions to be made on the ninth.

There were no panzer divisions used in the invasions, but everything went like lightning war nevertheless. Denmark, a small country with a tiny army, was conquered in only four hours, by a motorized infantry brigade and a division of regular infantry that were landed from a ship and quickly moved inland. In Norway, troops were landed from ships at a number of port cities. Parachute troops rained down from the sky and captured a major airfield, at which German transport planes soon began to land, bringing troops. Airborne troops in planes landed outside Oslo, Norway's capital, and the city of 250,000 was quickly taken over.

But in some places, Norwegian army units fought hard, and the British sent warships to Norwegian waters as quickly as possible. At the port of Narvik, British destroyers and a battleship wiped out an entire group of German destroyers, and other German ships were sunk by British submarines and Royal Air

A PzKpfw II rolls down a Copenhagen street. Denmark fell to German forces in just four hours.

Force bombers. British and French troops were landed at several places along Norway's coast. However, more German soldiers were brought in, too, and as in Poland the *Luftwaffe* had air superiority in Norway's sky, leaving German planes free to bomb enemy troops and drop supplies to hard-pressed German units. By the third of May, most of the British and French troops had been forced to pull out of the country. A few Norwegian forces fought on for a time, but finally had to surrender. Although Germany had lost a lot of ships, the invasion was a major success and a bitter blow for the Allies.

Meanwhile, a new plan for the German invasion of France had been perfected. Unlike the previous plan, which had aimed merely at pushing back the French and British armies and capturing some coastal ports, this plan was designed to completely *destroy* the French Army and to force the British to withdraw from France and return to Britain. Largely the brainchild of General Erich von Manstein, a member of the German General Staff, it called for a fake "main" attack to be launched through the Netherlands and Belgium to draw the British and French forces toward a certain part of Belgium. But the real attack would smash down into France from a place the French would never expect, circling around behind them.

Hitler approved the plan and it became the official plan of attack for the German Army. It was known as *Sichelschnitte*, meaning "sickle slice," from the way grain was cut down by the old-fashioned farm tool known as a sickle. The German military leaders expected that by using this plan, their forces would slice through the French Army like a farmer cutting down wheat!

Chapter 7

THE LIGHTNING STRIKES

The Allies, France and Great Britain, now had 104 divisions, forming 9 armies divided into 3 Army Groups. Belgium and the Netherlands had another 30 divisions altogether, for a total of 134. Against this, the German Army had 136 divisions, formed into 7 armies divided into 3 Army Groups. The German forces included 10 panzer divisions with a total of about 2,500 tanks. The Allies had some 3,000 tanks. About 1,700 of these were divided up into battalions of 45, parceled out among the infantry divisions. Eight hundred were in the French light mechanized and cavalry divisions. The rest consisted of a British brigade of 100 big, slow, Matilda tanks, and several hundred French light and heavy tanks in three armored divisions that had just been formed and were being held in reserve. In aircraft, the Allies had 1,835 bombers and 690 fighter planes, and Belgium and the Netherlands could put another 159 fighters into the air, to raise the total of those to 849. However, Germany had 1,210 fighters and 1,600 bombers, including the dreaded *Stuka* dive-bombers.

At 4:30 on the morning of May 10, 1940, flights of *Luftwaffe* bombers and fighter planes roared up from German airfields and sped off to strike like a whirlwind at military airports throughout the Netherlands, Belgium, and northern France. Half of the little Dutch Air Force of 125 planes was caught on the ground and destroyed. The bombers also hit railroad centers and bridges that might be of use to Allied forces, demolishing many of them.

As the sky lightened, scores of German Ju–52 transport planes began to drone across the border of the Netherlands. Soon, puffs of white were blossoming in the gray sky as parachutes opened and German paratroopers floated down from the planes onto key targets in the Dutch countryside—bridges, airfields, and road centers. The paratroops seized their objectives and hung on, beating off attacks by Dutch soldiers, until numbers of transport planes began to land, disgorging masses of soldiers of the German 22nd Air Landing Division. This was the first major airborne attack in the history of warfare.

By now, German ground troops were pouring across the border, headed by the 9th Panzer Division with 229 tanks. The small Dutch army was soon forced to retreat into the north, where there were many rivers and canals, some of which were now blocked so that they would flood, and create barriers against the German forces. But the German airborne troops still held the bridges across many of these waterways, and the movement of the German divisions could not be halted. The Germans began to curl around the Dutch forces, cutting them off from any help.

Belgium was hit at the same time. In Belgium the main target was a huge fortress, called Eben Emael, that blocked the way into the country. In the morning darkness, nine small gliders, launched from tow planes that passed overhead, and each carrying a small group of German airborne troops, came whispering down to land on *top* of Eben Emael. With explosive devices

In the first major airborne attack in the history of warfare, German paratroopers landed in Holland on May 10, 1940.

the German soldiers demolished the fort's guns and rendered the fort useless. Meanwhile, other gliders had landed in the area, and three hundred German troops seized bridges and vital points. Before long, German tanks were thundering into Belgium, pushing the Belgian Army out of the way.

At 7:00 in the morning, the Allied commander, General Gamelin gave the order for French and British forces to move up into Belgium according to plan. Five armies swung northward, forming a line that reached from the Belgian coast down to the edge of the Maginot Line, where another army was stationed. Stretched out behind the Maginot Line, in France, was a line of four more armies, and behind the armies in Belgium

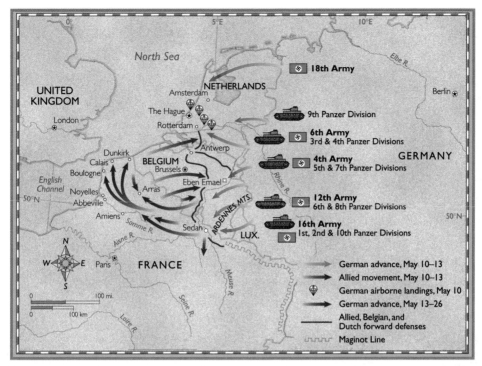

Sichelschnitte *("Sickle Slice")*

was a great reserve (reinforcement) force of fourteen divisions, including three light mechanized divisions and the three heavy armored divisions, ready to be sent forward whenever and wherever needed. Everything seemed to be in excellent shape. General Gamelin was seen smiling and humming a military march, as if completely confident.

But, of course, where the Allies were now was exactly where the German Army's *Sichelschnitte* plan wanted them. All was now ready for launching the *real* main attack. Even as French troops were marching northward to get into position in Belgium, Heinz Guderian's dream, an army of tanks, was rolling into France behind them. It had come through the one place that the French had believed it *couldn't* come through, the vast thick Ardennes Forest on the northern edge of the Maginot Line.

At the same time that bombers and fighter planes of the *Luftwaffe* were rising from airfields at dawn on the morning of

French military leaders never imagined that German tanks could come through the Ardennes, invading France by going around the forts of the Maginot Line.

May 10, the leading vehicles of the world's first tank army began rumbling up the road that led through the Ardennes Forest. In the early morning darkness the gray tanks were hulking black shapes. The crosses painted on them, identifying them as German, were no longer white as they had been in Poland, but were now black with a white edge.

The tank army stretched along the road for nearly a hundred miles. It was formed of 5 panzer divisions—1,264 tanks—and 3 motorized infantry divisions, all organized into 3 corps. The largest corps, the 19th, contained three panzer divisions plus an additional motorized infantry regiment, and was commanded by Heinz Guderian. The entire army was commanded by General Ewald von Kleist.

The 1st Panzer Division of Guderian's corps led von Kleist's army into the Ardennes, and Guderian was up near the front, as was his custom. The tanks were crowded together on the narrow road, and had to move slowly. If a tank or other vehicle broke down, as some did, it was quickly pushed off the road to one side. Overhead circled scores of German fighter planes, protecting the column of tanks from being seen by any Allied plane that might come into the area.

At about 5:30, the leading units of the 1st Panzer Division entered the tiny country of Luxembourg, which had no army and offered no resistance. But at around noon, the division crossed the border into Belgium and began to encounter chopped-down trees lying across the road, blown-up bridges, and even sections of road that had been destroyed with explosive charges. This had been done by a few small units of Belgian infantry that were the only defenders of the region, and who were now forced to drop back in the face of the oncoming German tanks. Working quickly, German soldiers removed the obstacles, constructed temporary bridges, or provided short detours, so that the tanks could rumble on.

As part of the movement into Belgium ordered by General Gamelin, four French cavalry divisions and two cavalry brigades went into the Ardennes on the tenth of May, to scout— horsemen armed with rifles, and light tanks and armored cars armed with machine guns. These units began to run into the leading German tanks and armored cars, which were more than they could handle, and they pulled back. With nothing to stop them, the panzer divisions pushed on, and by six o'clock on the morning of May 12, the 1st Panzer Division rolled into France. Thus, the Maginot Line, designed and built to prevent a German invasion of France, had turned out to be useless. The German forces had simply gone around it!

The first big obstacle the Germans would have to overcome on French soil was the wide, deep, Meuse River. All French forces in the area had withdrawn across the Meuse, blown up all

Belgian infantry units tried to slow the German invasion by blocking roads with fallen trees. Here, German soldiers clear the way for a PzKpfw III.

the bridges over it, and were trying to get into position on the other side to hold off the Germans when they arrived, until help could come. The French generals felt there was plenty of time to get ready. They agreed the German troops would probably not arrive for several days, and then it would surely take several more days, perhaps even a week, for them to bring up their artillery. That was how long it would have taken the French army.

But the French generals had never experienced lightning war. To their consternation, General Guderian's panzer divisions reached the Meuse on the evening of May 12, arriving at the city of Sedan. And they had everything they needed with them. Immediately, they began to prepare an assault.

At eleven o'clock the next morning the air was shattered as panzer division artillery opened up, pouring down a merciless rain of fire upon the French troops dug in on the opposite bank of the river. Only moments later the *Stuka*s appeared, called in by General Guderian, and the French soldiers received their first experience of dive-bombing. It went on for almost five straight hours as squadron after squadron of the bombers arrived one after another. The French soldiers cowered in their trenches, unable to even fire their weapons as the infantrymen of the 1st Panzer Division crossed the river on inflated rubber boats and began to move forward against them. Things were happening with incredible speed and violence, and the French troops simply could not stand up to them. Most of the *poilus* here were reservists, not full-time soldiers, and the terrifying *Stuka* attacks plus the realization that they would soon face an onslaught of hundreds of tanks was too much for them. They began to crumble before the fury of the *Blitzkrieg*. The French 55th Division literally came apart as men threw down their weapons and began to flee, leaving a great hole in the French line of defense.

Working speedily and efficiently through the night, panzer division engineers constructed a tank bridge across the river. By early morning of the next day, tanks of Guderian's 1st and 10th panzer divisions were fanning out on the opposite riverbank. A French counterattack by a battalion of forty-five French light tanks and an infantry regiment was beaten off. And then, with the German tanks bearing down on them, another division of French reservists, the 71st, collapsed and fled. The hole in the French defenses was now a gaping wound!

Chapter 8

THE TRIUMPH OF THE TANKS

The German panzer divisions were now in action everywhere. In Belgium, on May 12, the German 14th Corps, of two panzer divisions with a total of 623 tanks, encountered two French light mechanized divisions with 348 tanks. The first major tank battle of World War II erupted. It lasted all day, with neither side gaining the upper hand, but it served to show how the German and French tanks compared to each other. The German force outnumbered the French almost two to one, but 269 of the German tanks were the little PzKpfw I's, armed with only machine guns that could not even penetrate French tank armor. The German tanks armed with 20mm and 37mm anti-tank guns had to get very close to an enemy tank before they could do any damage, but the 47mm guns of the French S–35 tanks punched right through the armor of every kind of German tank from more than half a mile away. However, the French tanks did not have radio sets as the German tanks did, so they all had to move on their own, whereas German tanks moved in groups under the command of a leader.

The battle resumed on the morning of the next day, but now the Germans began taking advantage of what they had learned. Like packs of wolves hunting an elk, small groups of German tanks would close in on a single French tank and destroy it. Gradually, the French divisions weakened, and as night fell the French commander ordered his forces to withdraw. The French had lost 105 tanks and the Germans 164, but many of the German losses were the little PzKpfw I's, and the Germans still outnumbered the French considerably.

Farther south in Belgium, the 7th Panzer Division, commanded by Major General Erwin Rommel, had reached the Meuse River on the twelfth of May, and the division's motorcycle battalion had managed to get across the river by the next day. The battalion held its ground in the face of stiff French resistance, even beating off an attack by French light tanks. Meanwhile, the panzer division's sweating engineers, taking heavy casualties from French fire, constructed a bridge, and by twilight the German tanks were crossing the river. Desperate French attacks were beaten off, and by the morning of the fourteenth Rommel's division had established a firm "bridgehead"—full control of a section of river over which German forces could steadily advance.

Thus, by the end of the day on May 14, the German panzer units across the Meuse were building up for a breakthrough; a movement to cut through French forces and get behind them. Furthermore, on the evening of the fourteenth the Dutch Army surrendered, which left all the German troops in the Netherlands now free to move down into Belgium. Things were getting very serious for the Allies.

The French commanders desperately scrambled to do something to stop the relentless movement of the panzers, but they still did not understand the full scope of lightning war and they simply couldn't move fast enough. The French 3rd Armored Division was ordered forward from the reserve to counterattack Guderian's 1st Division, but by the time it arrived, Guderian's panzers were moving off in a different direction. As a result, instead of being kept together as a powerful fighting force, like a panzer division, the 3rd Division was broken up into many little groups to search for the enemy.

Another French armored division, the 1st, was sent to block the movement of Rommel's 7th Panzer Division. But one morning when it halted to refuel its tanks, Rommel's division and the 5th Panzer Division suddenly struck with guns blazing and support from *Stukas*. A daylong tank battle erupted, and by the day's end the French division was in flight, with only 50 of its 175 tanks left. Other units from the French reserve force were also simply wasted, either by being too late or by being thrown into battle against forces that were too much for them.

The French infantry in the path of the 5th and 7th panzer divisions now began to collapse in terror, just as those in the path of Guderian's tanks had done. Four infantry divisions, more than 67,000 men, simply ran away or surrendered. The gap in the French line between the armies in Belgium and those behind the Maginot Line was now more than 60 miles wide. Through this enormous hole swept Rommel's 7th Division with the 5th close behind. Von Kleist's entire tank army, with General Guderian's 1st, 2nd, and 10th panzer divisions in the lead, were all moving behind the shaken Allied forces, speeding toward the coast. The breakthrough had happened! And as the tanks moved forward, the gray-clad German infantry divisions came marching in behind them, to take possession of the territory the tanks had conquered.

The French High Command was now in near panic. General Gamelin ordered the Allied forces in Belgium to retreat, which they began to do on the night of May 16. Gamelin phoned the minister of defense (a position similar to U.S. secretary of defense) and told him that the French Army was "finished." Everyone expected Paris to soon be occupied by

German troops, and workers in government offices began burning secret documents and records, to keep them from falling into German hands.

However, the German panzer generals, Guderian, Rommel, and the others, were not concerned with trying to capture Paris. It was far more important, they knew, to keep speeding on to the coast. On May 20, Guderian's 2nd Panzer Division reached the city of Abbeville, only two miles from the sea. All the main roads coming down from the north led into Abbeville, which meant that Allied forces trying to retreat from Belgium were on roads that led directly to a place held by German troops. In other words, the Allied armies in Belgium were now trapped!

The other panzer divisions continued their rush toward the coast, intent on capturing vital ports and cutting off any chance that some of the trapped Allied forces could escape by sea. Guderian's divisions managed to take the ports of Boulogne and Calais from the French and British troops defending them, and meanwhile the German forces in Belgium were able to push between the Belgian army and the British and French forces. By the twenty-fifth of May the Allied armies were surrounded.

The British and French troops began pulling toward the town of Dunkirk, the only seaport left to them. With the German armies closing in around them, they were faced with either having to surrender or being wiped out. Thus, Great Britain was now in desperate danger of losing almost its entire army, which would leave Britain helpless against a German invasion. So, the British government determined that its troops and as many French troops as possible should be taken out of Dunkirk by sea, in what would be the largest troop evacuation (pullout) by sea in history. It was actually too big a job for even the British Navy to do by itself, so throughout Britain, owners of boats and small ships of every size were asked to volunteer their crafts and themselves to help save the British Army.

Allied troops line the beaches and wade in the sea as the evacuation of Dunkirk gets underway.

General Guderian's panzer corps was fighting its way up the coast toward Dunkirk, and other panzer units were closing in on the town as well. Suddenly, the German High Command ordered them all to halt. Apparently, Adolf Hitler had decided to try to let the *Luftwaffe* destroy the British and French forces in Dunkirk by means of bombing raids. From where they had stopped, the troops of Guderian's panzer divisions could see the huge number of ships of all sizes, from warships to fishing boats, spread out in the harbor, each one taking on as many soldiers as it could hold. The town, the beach around it, and the ships in the water were all under constant artillery fire and bombing attacks by *Stuka*s and other bombers. Bombs and cannon shells had ignited a cluster of oil tanks, and the whole town appeared to be on fire, wrapped in billowing clouds of black smoke. Wrecks of ships destroyed by bombs cluttered the harbor. Lines of men waiting to get aboard ships stood in the water, some up to their necks. German fighter planes often swooped down to rake them with chattering machine guns.

Every inch of space was used on the vessels that took part in the operation at Dunkirk—the largest troop evacuation by sea in history.

But despite the awful destruction, most of the British troops and many of the French troops as well did manage to get away. After two days the panzers were ordered to attack Dunkirk, but by then it was too late for the smashing victory that the tanks might have achieved—the capture of the entire British army in France. About 338,000 British and French soldiers had been removed from Dunkirk and taken safely to Britain, to become the basis of a new army to fight against Hitler.

However, the British Army was now gone from France, and on May 28 the Belgian Army surrendered. The French forces remaining in the Dunkirk area were wiped out or taken prisoner; a loss of twenty-four infantry divisions, two cavalry divisions, three light mechanized divisions, and one heavy armored division. Thus, a badly crippled France now stood totally alone, and the German Army prepared to launch the final onslaught that would utterly shatter it.

Chapter 9

THE FALL OF FRANCE

General Gamelin was removed as commander of the French forces and his place was taken by General Maxim Weygand, a seventy-three-year old man who had been a hero of World War I for the French people. Weygand produced a plan and gave orders to put what was left of his army into position to try to fight off the German attack.

Two rivers, the Somme and the Aisne, flow through northwestern France, just below the Belgian border. With the sixty-some divisions he had left, Weygand formed a line of five armies that stretched 225 miles behind the rivers, from the coast to the Maginot Line. Another three small armies were grouped behind the Maginot Line, which was still manned by fortress troops.

Poised on the other side of the rivers were the German forces that had conquered the Netherlands, Belgium, and northern France; 140 divisions including the 10 panzer divisions. Facing the Maginot Line was the German Army Group "C," of nineteen divisions that had been waiting there menacingly since the tenth of May.

The new German attack, called *Fall Rot* ("Operation Red")

The German invasion of France, a triumph of "lightning war" tactics, took only 43 days. In this photograph, German tanks roll down a street in a French town two days before France surrenders.

began on the fifth of June, as six panzer divisions exploded across the Somme River and smashed into the French positions. Four days later, a tank army of four panzer divisions and two motorized infantry divisions, commanded by General Guderian, who had now been given the nickname *Der Schnelle Heinz* ("Speedy" Heinz) by his men, roared across the Aisne River. Behind these armored spearheads came waves of infantry.

The French troops fought hard and well, but the battle was really over before it even began. The French were simply spread too thin and were too badly outnumbered. Two of the panzer divisions, the 5th and Rommel's 7th, swung to their right and pushed two of Weygand's divisions up against the coast, where they were forced to surrender. Four others broke through the French lines and headed toward Paris. Guderian's tanks sliced through the French forces in front of them and sped toward the Swiss border, moving behind the three French armies at the Maginot Line, cutting them off from any help.

June 14 was a day of humiliation for France. As citizens of Paris watched, many of them in tears, masses of German soldiers marched through the city in a giant victory parade. The capital of France was in German hands. And on the same day, the German First Army, of Army Group "C," struck across the border at the "impenetrable" Maginot Line, and without using a single tank, broke right through it! The German soldiers had discovered that there were "blind spots" in the fortifications, where the defenders could not see what was coming at them from the side. With flamethrowers and explosive charges, the German infantrymen demolished enough of the defenses so that troops were able to come pouring through. France's pride, the Maginot Line, had now been revealed as totally useless. The Germans had invaded France by simply going around it, and now the Maginot Line had not done the main thing it had been built to do—keep the Germans from coming right through.

The end was now at hand. With a flood of infantry coming at them through the Maginot Line and Guderian's panzers threatening them from behind, the three French armies behind the Maginot Line surrendered. And on the twenty-second of June, the entire French nation surrendered.

The news of the fall of France and the near destruction of the British army was an incredible, stunning shock to the United States, Canada, and other free nations. The "unbreakable" Maginot Line had been easily broken, and the "world's best army" had been totally shattered in only forty-three days! The word *Blitzkrieg* was now known throughout the world as the name for a new kind of incredibly fast-moving, savagely effective warfare.

But actually, the day of the *Blitzkrieg* was over. In June 1941, the forces of Germany once again launched a lightning attack with four panzer armies in the forefront, into Russia. At first, it seemed a repeat of Poland and France, as the German tanks raced deep into Russian territory, inflicting thousands of casualties and steadily pushing the Soviet forces in their path out of the way. But then, things began to change. The Soviet Union had watched how Germany had fought its wars in Poland and France, and had learned. It, too, had tank armies, and with a

The fall of Paris, on June 14, 1940, was a stunning blow to the people of France. In this photograph, a German tank stands before the Arc de Triomphe.

tank that was actually better than any of the German tanks. The German advance was brought to a halt and gradually pushed back.

The British and others had also learned from the Germans. In North Africa, German tank forces under the command of Erwin Rommel fought against a British Army that also used tanks as a main weapon. And when the United States Army went into combat against Germany, it, too, had armored divisions, containing some of the best tanks in the world. The day of the *Blitzkrieg* was over because Germany's opponents now understood the methods of lightning war, and had weapons to wage it themselves.

Thus, the lightning war developed by the German Army at the beginning of World War II changed the way that wars were to be fought from then on. Tanks, those clumsy machines that most generals had sneered at after World War I, had now become the main weapon of all the world's armies. The tactics that armies use today, with fast-moving, well-armed tanks, mobilized infantry and artillery, and close support from helicopter gunships and missile-armed aircraft, are based upon the tactics of the lightning war carried out by the German panzer divisions that roared through Poland, Belgium, the Netherlands, and France, more than half a century ago.

Index

Page numbers in *italics* refer to illustrations.